THE FIGHT FOR EQUAL RIGHTS

"BLOODY TUESDAY"

MARLISA WIGGINS

THE FIGHT FOR EQUAL RIGHTS
Marlisa Wiggins

Illustrator: Prabir - India

Printed in the United States of America
Keen Vision Publishing, LLC
www.publishwithkvp.com
ISBN: 979-8-9927392-1-3

Dedicated to the local Black citizens of Tuscaloosa and the surrounding areas who marched for my generation and the generations to follow. I also posthumously dedicate this book to the memory of Theophilus Yelverton Rogers, Jr., affectionately known as T. Y. Rogers.

Special thanks to Fisher Liam for keeping me focused on this task.

On January 1, 1863, President Abraham Lincoln declared that all enslaved people be freed, but nearly 100 years later, Blacks were still ensnared in Jim Crow practices all over the United States.

Many Blacks in Alabama were being victimized and murdered by whites, and segregation had won. Blacks were not allowed the same rights or privileges as their white counterparts. They had to dine in different areas and could not have the same opportunities as whites.

Blacks were not safe in Alabama. In Birmingham, four girls were killed at 16th Street Baptist Church on September 15, 1963, as a result of racial motivation. Many Black families lost loved ones due to racism. This behavior was sadly common during this time.

In Tuscaloosa, west of Birmingham, Alabama, known for its vicious treatment of Blacks, the proud African American citizens had had enough of being treated like second-class citizens. They decided they were going to make a change.

Welcome to
Tuscaloosa
Enough
is
Enough!
Equality
for All

The citizens began having mass meetings at First African Baptist Church under the leadership of Reverend Theophilus Yelverton Rogers, Jr., affectionately known as T.Y., to decide how they would gain fair treatment and equal rights.

Appointed by Martin Luther King, Jr., T.Y. could move his congregation with his words and actions. He, along with the black citizens of Tuscaloosa, contemplated multiple ways not to support local businesses that were racist so unlawful practices could end.

They pondered multiple ideas of how to be treated as true citizens. They even thought of boycotting the purchase of Christmas trees, but that would have hurt their children. Finally, the decision was made. There would be a peaceful march to the newly built courthouse. T.Y. told them to "bring their toothbrush." They would need to be ready to spend a long time away from home as they protested.

The Black citizens were promised that the courthouse would not have segregated bathrooms and drinking fountains; however, this was not the truth.

COURTHOUSE
BLACK ONLY
WHITE ONLY

Rev. T.Y. Rogers, along with the courageous Blacks, met at First African Baptist Church for prayer before they entered Tuscaloosa's brutal streets.

On June 9, 1964, the Blacks reconvened at First African Baptist Church. They sang spirituals, and when the spirit was high, they marched out of the church.

As they left the church with a goal to protest the courthouse peacefully, they were met with severe violence from the police and Klansmen. The courageous Black citizens were hit with billy clubs and rocks as they began to exit the church. The violence spilled onto the streets, where tear gas was used to control them.

Some of the citizens were beaten, thrown into paddy wagons, and sent to jail. Some received aid at a local barbershop. This siege lasted 45 minutes. Many Blacks, young and old, were taken to jail. Maxie Thomas, a 21-year-old man, was among the Blacks beaten and thrown into jail.

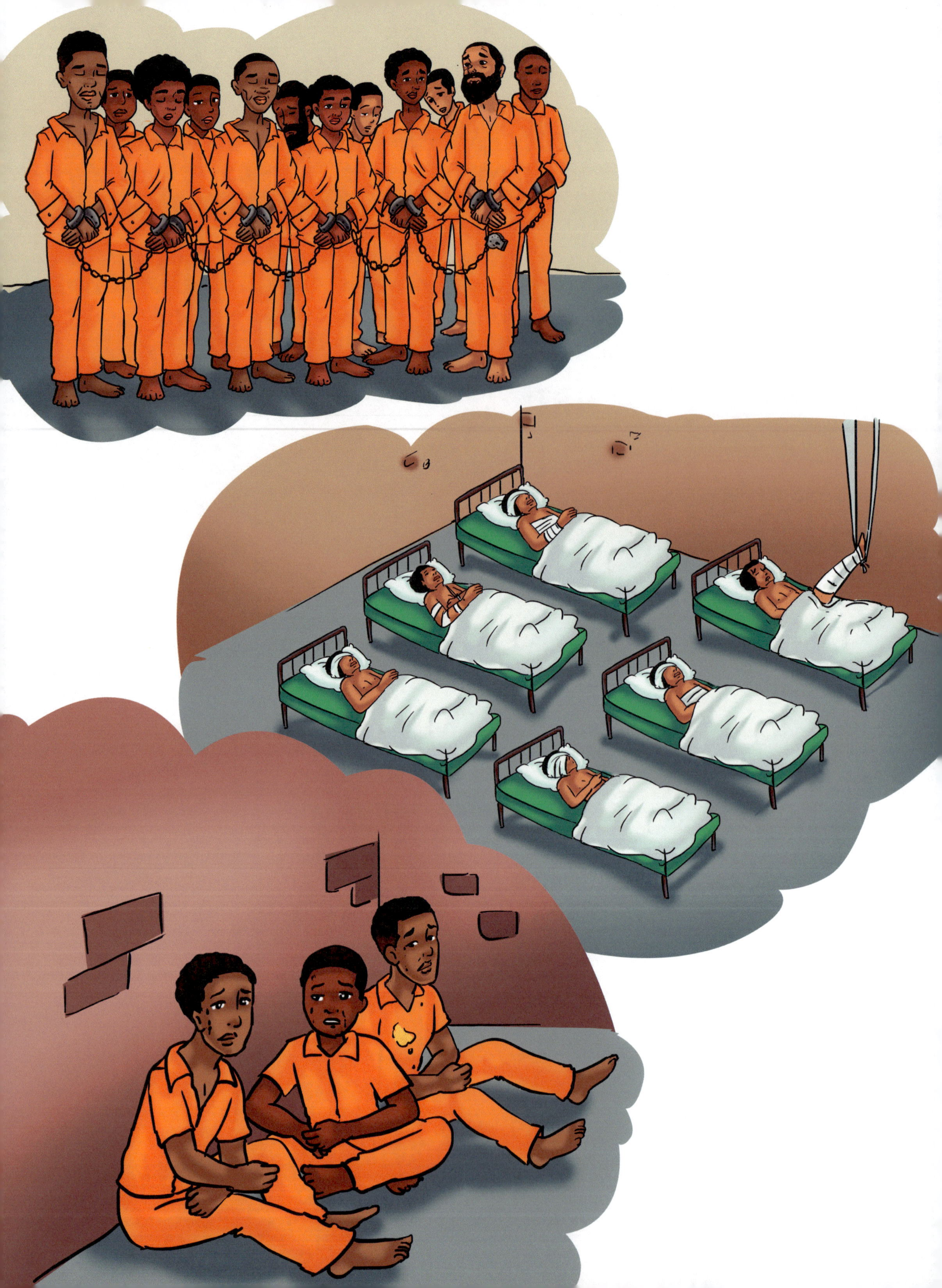

Over 90 people were arrested, 33 were hospitalized, and dozens had cuts and bruises during this demonstration, but this event was never recorded in Tuscaloosa's local newspaper.

Over 500 citizens, including Stillman College students, participated in this brutal event. Some names like Odessa Warrick, Irene I. Byrd, Jerry Martin, Danny Steele, Olivia White, George Crummie, John Byrd, McDonald Hughes, Howard Linton, Charles Steele, Maude Whatley, and Jimmy Hardaway have not been forgotten.

Their efforts, plus the hundreds of others who participated, changed Tuscaloosa. The event, dubbed "Bloody Tuesday" by the survivors, was the beginning of change for the Blacks. Their persistence in the movement slashed Jim Crow laws, and this event, along with multiple events around the South, ended racist practices in public places.

VICTORY!
Black Only
White Only

ABOUT THE AUTHOR

Marlisa Wiggins is a devoted English teacher from Tuscaloosa, Alabama, with a deep-seated passion for history. Her fascination with Tuscaloosa's local African American history ignited unexpectedly while watching a news segment about civil rights demonstrations that had occurred right in her hometown — events she had never known about. This revelation led to profound discussions with her parents and countless hours spent watching historical footage, drawing her ever deeper into the stories of her community.

Marlisa's book, *The Fight for Equality: Bloody Tuesday*, is born from a desire to shed light on these critical yet overlooked events in Tuscaloosa's history. As an educator, she aims to enlighten and inform those who, like herself, were unaware of the significant struggles and triumphs that occurred on their own streets. Through her engaging narrative, Marlisa seeks to educate her readers, inspiring them to appreciate the complex tapestry of human rights and the ongoing journey towards equality.

Made in the USA
Columbia, SC
24 May 2025